Original title:
Geometry of Dreams

Copyright © 2024 Creative Arts Management OÜ
All rights reserved.

Author: Clement Portlander
ISBN HARDBACK: 978-9916-88-066-1
ISBN PAPERBACK: 978-9916-88-067-8

The Cartography of Consciousness

In the mind's vast expanse, we wander,
Drawing maps with threads of thought.
Each path a vivid memory,
Each turn a lesson taught.

Whispers of dreams in the twilight,
Guide us through the starlit haze.
Unraveling the maze of worry,
Finding peace in gentle ways.

Layers of feelings intertwine,
A tapestry of joy and pain.
Navigating through the chaos,
In hope, we find our gain.

With every heartbeat, we discover,
New realms within our beating chest.
The cartography of existence,
Leads us toward our rightful quest.

Lattice of Luminosity

In the night, a web of stars,
Glistening threads of pure delight.
A lattice woven with whispers,
Illuminating paths of light.

Every glimmer tells a story,
Of dreams that dance in cosmic play.
Threads of hope and fleeting shadows,
Marking where our wishes sway.

Radiance breaks the heavy silence,
Painting hues on canvases rare.
In the lattice, we find solace,
A refuge in the open air.

As the dawn begins to shimmer,
The lattice glows with new designs.
In every strand, a breath of promise,
Emerging where the sunlight shines.

Celestial Symmetry

Stars align in silent night,
Whispers weave in silver light.
Galaxies dance in cosmic grace,
Time stands still in vast embrace.

Stardust falls like gentle rain,
Dreams are born, we feel no pain.
Planets spin in endless flow,
Hearts ignite with every glow.

Dreamscapes in Pixelated Form

Colors blur in twilight hue,
Pixels form a world so new.
Journey through a glowing screen,
Lost in realms where we've not been.

Fingers tap on keys so light,
Crafting stories in the night.
Fantasy blooms with every click,
Fragments dance, both swift and thick.

A Tangle of Thoughts

Whirls of mind in chaos spun,
Seeking peace where dreams begun.
Threads entwine with softest grace,
In this maze, we find our place.

Whispers call from deep within,
Waves of doubt beneath the skin.
Casting nets to catch the stars,
In the dark, we mend our scars.

Lattice of Longing

Woven dreams in twilight's thread,
Hearts entwined, where hope is bred.
Yearning glows in shadows cast,
Echoes linger, hold us fast.

Through the lattice, visions grow,
Every whisper, soft and slow.
Fields of longing, wild and free,
In this maze, we find our key.

Rhythms of the Universe

In the night, the echoes play,
Stars will sway, stars will sway.
Galaxies dance in endless flight,
Cosmic whispers trace the night.

Planets turn, their secrets keep,
Mysteries in every sweep.
Waves of light in colors bright,
Guide the hearts towards the light.

Harmonies of the Hidden

In shadows deep, a song will rise,
Nature hums, and silence sighs.
Leaves will rustle, rivers flow,
Magic weaves in sounds we know.

Each heartbeat echoes tales untold,
Layers of life, both young and old.
In every breath, a tale confined,
Harmony in paths entwined.

Traced by Stars

Each starlit path leads to dreams,
History whispers through their beams.
Travelers gaze in awe and bliss,
Each twinkle shaped by fate's soft kiss.

Constellations guide the lost,
In the sky, they count the cost.
Ancient maps in cosmic ink,
In their light, our spirits sink.

Spirals of Imagination

In a mind where visions twirl,
Thoughts unfurl, colors whirl.
Ideas bloom like flowers rare,
Endless paths we dream and dare.

Through the spiral, journeys bend,
With each turn, new worlds to send.
Imagination's flight is free,
Creating realms for you and me.

The Illusion of Measure

In whispers soft, the shadows play,
Time bends and sways, then slips away.
We count the hours, yet lose the sum,
In silent rooms where nothing's done.

Each tick a brush, an artist's sigh,
Painting the moments as they fly.
Yet in this canvas, we find no peace,
Just fleeting glimpses that never cease.

Figures Dancing in the Dark

Beneath the moon's ethereal glow,
Figures twirl in a silent flow.
With every step, the shadows blend,
Creating stories that never end.

A dance of echoes, a soft refrain,
In the night's embrace, they feel no pain.
Lost in the rhythm, they sway and spin,
Chasing the dreams that lie within.

Labyrinth of Echoes

In twisted halls where secrets breathe,
Each whisper calls, a haunting wreathe.
Footsteps falter, a heartbeat loud,
In this maze where fears are bowed.

Mirrors trap what cannot stay,
Reflections twist and drift away.
The path is lost, yet voices guide,
Through the shadows where thoughts collide.

Reflections in a Prism

Light shatters, colors spill,
In fractured hues, they bend at will.
A thousand shades in vibrant flight,
Each a story, bold and bright.

In this spectrum, truths unfold,
Whispers of warmth, of stories told.
We chase the light, but never see,
The beauty lies in the mystery.

Routes of the Subconscious

Whispers in the dark, they guide,
Through winding paths, feelings collide.
A hidden realm, shadows sway,
Lost in the maze where dreams play.

Echoes of laughter, memories blend,
Time bends and twists, a mind to mend.
In quiet corners, secrets bloom,
Flickering fireflies, lighting the room.

Fragments of life, drifting away,
Tangled threads in bright dismay.
Reality dims, the dreamers flow,
Finding the truths only few know.

Awake in the night, visions soar,
Unlocking doors to evermore.
Through labyrinthine routes, we find,
The deepest depths of the mind.

Spheres of Serenity

In tranquil pools, reflections gleam,
Guardians of peace, they softly beam.
Gentle breezes, whispers so light,
Calming the chaos, embracing the night.

Beneath the trees, a sanctuary grows,
Every petal falling, a story that flows.
Softly the river sings to the stones,
In its warm current, we find our tones.

Stars like lanterns in the vast skyscape,
Guiding the weary, offering escape.
Within the spheres where spirits connect,
An endless embrace, all hearts reflect.

Harmony found in every breath,
Easing the tension, defying death.
In spheres of serenity, peace resides,
Where each soul wanders, and love abides.

Abstract Narratives

In colors so bright, a tale unfolds,
Brushstrokes whisper, the heart beholds.
Each canvas lives, stories collide,
Emotions trapped, nowhere to hide.

Shadows dance on the gallery wall,
Memories echo, both big and small.
Fragments of time, splintered yet whole,
A vivid reflection of the elusive soul.

Words unsaid linger in the air,
Expressions captured, a glimpse, a stare.
Narratives shift in the light of the mind,
A maze of perception, no end to find.

In abstract depths, we lose and bind,
In every stroke, a reason to find.
Every silence holds a voice yet to speak,
In art's embrace, the heart feels meek.

The Tessellation of Thought

Patterns emerging, pieces align,
In the puzzle of mind, we intertwine.
Each thought a tile, a story to tell,
In intricate designs, we rise and fell.

Colors merge, the edges blend,
Fractals of memory, never to end.
A symmetry born from chaos and time,
In the dance of reason, we search for rhyme.

Layers of meaning folded so close,
Unraveling threads, a delicate dose.
Through space and silence, ideas arise,
In the tessellation, truth never lies.

Crafted creations, a labyrinth wide,
Each twist and turn a journey inside.
In the tessellation of thought we weave,
A tapestry rich, in which we believe.

The Weave of Wishes

In twilight's glow, dreams softly thread,
A tapestry of hopes, where hearts are led.
Each whisper lingers, woven with care,
In the loom of fate, they dance in the air.

Threads of sorrow, hues of delight,
Entwine in the darkness, ignite the night.
A fragile balance, both twisted and strong,
In this sweet silence, we all belong.

Beneath the stars, our secrets reside,
In the fabric of time, where wishes abide.
Fleeting moments, captured like dew,
In the weave of wishes, I find you too.

So let us spin, with laughter and grace,
In this grand design, we find our place.
With every heartbeat, the thread grows tight,
Together we shine, our spirits alight.

Points of Departure

From every ending, a journey begins,
With courage and hope, we rise through the din.
A compass of dreams, where paths intertwine,
In fleeting moments, our destinies shine.

Footprints in sand, washed by the tide,
Marking the places where we once cried.
Embrace the unknown, let go of the past,
In the dance of life, we find peace at last.

Bridges of trust span the rivers of time,
With every heartbeat, a rhythm, a rhyme.
We gather our thoughts, like stars in the sky,
In the points of departure, together we fly.

So let us embark on this voyage anew,
With hearts full of wonder, and skies painted blue.
For every point reached, another does call,
In the tapestry of life, we discover it all.

Interstellar Patterns

Stars map the sky in intricate patterns,
A cosmic dance that never flattens.
Galaxies swirl, secrets they share,
In the silence of space, we breathe the air.

Each moment a spark, igniting the dark,
In the vastness of night, we find our mark.
Celestial whispers guide us along,
In the rhythm of cosmos, we feel strong.

Nebulae bloom in colors so rare,
Painting the heavens with tender care.
Threads of existence, entwined we roam,
In interstellar patterns, we find our home.

So gaze at the stars, let your spirit soar,
Amongst these wonders, forever explore.
For in the universe's endless embrace,
We trace our journeys through time and space.

The Expanse of Wishes

In the expanse of wishes, dreams take flight,
Drifting like clouds, soft and light.
Each hope a feather, gliding with grace,
In the deep of the night, we find our place.

Beneath the moon, we whisper our dreams,
Carried away on silvery streams.
A symphony echoes through shadows and light,
In the expanse of wishes, everything feels right.

Stars twinkle brightly, our secrets they keep,
While we chase the echoes that linger in sleep.
The universe opens, a canvas so wide,
In the expanse of wishes, love is our guide.

So let us paint with colors so bright,
In the tapestry woven from day into night.
With every wish cast, our spirits entwine,
In the expanse of wishes, forever we shine.

Patterns woven in Starlight

In the dark, a tapestry lies,
Woven with whispers, soft sighs.
Stars twinkle, a cosmic delight,
Painting dreams in the night.

Threads of silver, golds so bright,
Dancing gently, pure and light.
Patterns swirl in celestial grace,
A universe spun, a timeless space.

Each twinkle tells a story old,
Secrets of galaxies, bold.
Patterns shift and gently play,
Guiding lost souls on their way.

In the silence, beauty grows,
Echoes of laughter, softly flows.
Beneath the vast, enchanted dome,
The starlit sky feels like home.

The Architecture of Fantasy

Castles rise from dreams of lore,
Built on whispers from yore.
Towers stretch to kiss the skies,
Bathed in magic, where hope lies.

Bridges arc in fragrant air,
Linking worlds beyond compare.
Windows gleam with visions bright,
Framed in shadows, kissed by light.

Chimeras roam on streets of gold,
Legends bask, as stories unfold.
Every corner, a new delight,
Created in the heart of night.

In this realm where wonders dwell,
All who enter, cast a spell.
Architecture of dreams still stands,
Crafted softly by our hands.

Lines that Bend and Break

In the sand, the lines do trace,
Curving soft, a delicate grace.
Waves might wash them out of sight,
Yet they reflect the will to fight.

Paths diverge, a puzzle spun,
Each turn whispers, "Life's begun."
Bend with time, don't stand so straight,
Embrace the curves, love your fate.

Fragile threads may snap in two,
But new ones blossom, fresh and true.
In the dance of fate, we bend,
Learning that we can transcend.

Emotions sway like tides that shift,
In every crack, we find a gift.
Lines may bend, or break away,
But strength resides in every sway.

Polygons of the Night

Shapes emerge from shadows deep,
In the night, where secrets keep.
Triangles dance in moonlit glade,
Casting spells that never fade.

Squares hold stories, edges sharp,
In quiet corners, whispers harp.
Circles spin, a gentle flow,
Binding hearts, where love will grow.

Hexagons of honeyed dreams,
Buzzing softly, drifting beams.
Each angle tells a tale anew,
Framing worlds that feel so true.

In these shapes, a magic thrives,
Awakening our hidden lives.
Polygons in the dark ignite,
Crafting wonders of the night.

Fluid Geometries

In waves of form, the colors blend,
Shapes that dance, and softly bend.
A symphony of lines, in motion bright,
Constructs of dreams, beyond our sight.

Curves entwine, in gentle grace,
Reflecting thought, in time and space.
The liquid art, a flowing thread,
Where logic sleeps, and vision's led.

Circles whisper, secrets spun,
Through fractal paths, where we've begun.
Fluid realms, where limits cease,
Embracing change, a silent peace.

In every turn, there's depth to find,
A geometry of the heart and mind.
Exploring worlds, both new and old,
In fluid shapes, our truths unfold.

The Structure of Sentience

In strands of thought, we weave our tale,
Fractured light, a whispering veil.
Conscious edges, sharp yet free,
The architecture of memory.

Layered minds, like rooms we build,
Emotions dance, and voices thrilled.
Connections pulse, with fervent spark,
An intricate map, both light and dark.

Time's observations, softly gleam,
Reflections captured, like a dream.
From silence flows, the music of now,
In the structure of thought, we take a bow.

Awareness blooms in shadow's light,
Crafting worlds from day to night.
Each heartbeat echoes, a sacred sign,
In the tapestry of mind, we intertwine.

Radiant Realities

In twilight hues, the visions rise,
A canvas stretched across the skies.
Colors burst, a vivid spree,
Radiance flows, a timeless sea.

A dance of stars, with secrets shared,
Softly glimmering, brightly bared.
Through shimmering glass, the worlds collide,
Infinite paths, with light as guide.

Perception shifts, like shifting sands,
In every heartbeat, the universe stands.
Moments captured in vibrant hue,
Painting truths in a world so new.

In radiant pulses, life expands,
Creating wonders with gentle hands.
Through luminous echoes, we roam and play,
Finding solace in the light of day.

Pathways to the Unknown

In labyrinths of thought we tread,
With every step, new worlds we spread.
Curiosity's spark ignites the night,
Illuminating paths, with hidden light.

Winding trails through misty dreams,
Where reason falters, and madness beams.
The heart of journeys, uncharted lands,
In whispers soft, the future stands.

Exploring realms, both dark and bright,
With courage found in the depths of fright.
Ever seeking truths, we venture far,
Guided by an inner star.

Each step a rhythm, a dance divine,
In the unknown, our spirits align.
Embracing change, embracing fear,
For in each path, new wonders appear.

Dreamscapes in Symmetry

In twilight hues, the shadows play,
Each corner bends, a dance ballet.
Whispers echo through the air,
Symmetry found, in dreams we share.

Reflections twist in silver light,
Chasing visions, soft as night.
Patterns weave through time and space,
In endless realms, we find our place.

The horizon glows with colors bright,
Opening doors to new delight.
With every breath, we float and glide,
Through dreamscapes vast, as tides abide.

Awake or slumber, we explore,
In symmetry's arms, we long for more.
Together lost, we'll find our fate,
In realms of dreams, we celebrate.

Polygons of the Heart

Shapes of love in every way,
Angles meet and gently sway.
Hearts collide like stars at night,
Creating patterns, pure and bright.

Triangles form with tender grace,
Each side carved, a warm embrace.
Squares of trust align so true,
Forms of passion, me and you.

In circles flow, the laughter sings,
While edges sharpen with the sting.
The math of us, a sacred art,
Mapping journeys, polygons of heart.

Together we sketch this vibrant tale,
With vibrant love that will not pale.
Through every shape, a story's told,
In polygons, our love unfolds.

The Architecture of Slumber

Beneath the stars, our dreams expand,
Blueprints drawn by fate's own hand.
Cathedrals rise in twilight's glow,
In slumber's reign, we come and go.

A fortress built of whispers sweet,
Where hopes and fears converge and meet.
Arches stretched across the night,
In this architecture, hearts take flight.

The walls are soft, a gentle hold,
Each brick a memory, bright as gold.
In corridors of silent grace,
We find our haven, find our place.

With every sigh, new visions bloom,
In slumber's house, we chase the moon.
Your hand in mine, we journey far,
Through architecture of who we are.

Mosaics of the Mind

Fragments shattered, colors bright,
Pieces lost in day and night.
Every thought a tiny shard,
In mosaics, life is hard.

Patterns emerge from chaos spun,
With every challenge, every run.
The beauty found in cracks and flaws,
Our minds create without a pause.

Layers blend, the old and new,
In vibrant hues, a dream comes true.
Stories told in every piece,
In this mosaic, we find peace.

Through every patch, a journey shared,
In the gallery of souls, we cared.
United minds in art divine,
Mosaics of the heart intertwine.

Infinity's Blueprint

In the vast expanse where dreams collide,
Stars and shadows in a dance abide.
Every line drawn, a story untold,
In the fabric of time, destinies unfold.

Imprints of moments lost in the swell,
Crafting a timeline where whispers dwell.
Waves of creation ripple through space,
Tracing existence in every embrace.

Patterns emerge like echoes of sound,
In the silence where secrets are found.
Blueprints of life, intricately spun,
In the realm of infinity, we are all one.

Shapes of the Night

Shadows emerge as the daylight fades,
Mysteries stir in the starry glades.
Forms etched in darkness, a silent feat,
Each angle whispers of secrets discreet.

Moonlight drapes over hills like a veil,
Caressing the night with a gentle tale.
Shapes intertwine in an elegant dance,
Guided by stars in their luminous trance.

Figures in twilight, a fleeting view,
Glimmers of dreams in shades of blue.
Every curve tracing paths of the heart,
In the canvas of night, art plays its part.

Whispering Angles

Angles converge where silence breathes,
In the quiet, a thousand leaves.
Whispers of light play tricks on the eye,
In the corners where shadows shy.

Patterns of thoughts amid spirals of grace,
Holding the secrets of time and space.
Every edge sharp, yet soft in the glow,
An echo of moments that ebb and flow.

Messages linger in delicate lines,
In the tapestry woven through old pine signs.
Here in the whispers, the world feels vast,
As angles unfold stories of the past.

Celestial Intersections

Where galaxies meet and collide in dance,
Time turns to magic in a cosmic trance.
Stars wink softly, their secrets set free,
In celestial meetings, infinity.

Paths intertwine like a lover's embrace,
In the starlit heavens, we find our place.
Nebulas blossom in colors untold,
In the space between dreams, new worlds unfold.

These intersections, a boundless affair,
Carving out stories in the midnight air.
Every moment a flicker, a bright constellation,
In the embrace of the universe's creation.

Aerial Blueprints

Silent skies above us roam,
Tracing paths where dreams will comb.
Hopes like kites on winds will rise,
In vivid hues beneath bright skies.

Each stitch in air a vision bright,
Drawing tales of day and night.
Plans that soar, ambitions great,
Sketching futures, shaping fate.

Clouds that whisper stories old,
Blueprints in the sun unfold.
Crafting realms both vast and wide,
With every thought, we build and guide.

Ethereal Ecosystems

In gardens where the spirits dwell,
Nature's whispers weave a spell.
Light cascades on emerald roots,
Life unfurls in gentle shoots.

Every creature plays a role,
Harmonies in perfect whole.
Softly singing, breezes play,
Echoing the dawn of day.

Colors burst in splendid show,
Flowing rivers, mountains grow.
In the heart of this embrace,
Nature's rhythm finds its place.

Vertex of Visions

At the peak where thoughts converge,
Ideas sparking, minds emerge.
Futures gleam like stars at night,
In the nexus, dreams take flight.

Angles sharp, perspectives vast,
Time suspends, the die is cast.
Crafting moments, chasing truth,
In the dawn, igniting youth.

With every glance, new paths we face,
Celebrating the sacred space.
Here at the vertex, we align,
Visions crafted, dreams divine.

Constructs of Clarity

In shadows deep, we seek the light,
Brick by brick, we shape our sight.
Towering thoughts reach for the sun,
Each layer built, a battle won.

Wisdom lays its strong foundation,
Crafting dreams, igniting passion.
In every gap, a lesson grows,
Through the chaos, purpose flows.

Structures rise with strength and grace,
In the quiet, we find our place.
With clarity, our hearts can see,
The beauty of what's meant to be.

Shapes in the Twilight

In the dusk, shadows play,
Figures dance in soft decay.
Harboring secrets of the night,
Whispers glide in fading light.

Silhouettes against the sky,
Twisted forms that drift and sigh.
Beneath the stars, they gently sway,
Lost in dreams, they float away.

Colors fade, yet linger still,
Painting visions, time to kill.
In twilight's grasp, we find our place,
A fleeting glimpse of hidden grace.

Echoes hum through the cool air,
Mysteries spun, an art laid bare.
As darkness weaves its velvet thread,
Shapes of twilight softly spread.

Fractal Whispers of the Mind

Thoughts unfurl like fractals bright,
Branches reaching, infinite light.
Patterns tangled, deep and vast,
Echoes of futures, shadows cast.

In every turn, a new delight,
Whispers twine in endless flight.
Lake reflections, ripples blend,
A journey with no start or end.

Curves and angles intertwined,
Fragments dance within the mind.
Fleeting visions, stories told,
In fractal dreams, we lose our hold.

Each pulse a clue, a hidden path,
Unraveling, we feel its wrath.
Yet, in chaos, order sings,
Fractal whispers grant us wings.

Coordinates of Reverie

In the map of dreams, we trace,
Coordinates in timeless space.
Points connect, a gentle arc,
Guiding hearts through realms so dark.

Through portals vast, we wander free,
Navigating what we cannot see.
Stars align to light the way,
In reverie, we long to stay.

Echoes of a distant song,
In whispers soft, we can belong.
Sketching paths with outstretched hands,
Creating worlds, we make our stands.

With every heartbeat, journeys start,
Coordinates etched within the heart.
In soft embrace of night's embrace,
We write our stories, time and space.

Angles of the Unseen

In corners where shadows kiss,
Angles hide in quiet bliss.
Perspective shifts, the eyes behold,
Stories whispered, truths unfold.

Lines intersect in gentle bends,
Where every echo softly ends.
Fractured light through broken seams,
Revealing layers of our dreams.

Sculpting edges with our gaze,
Finding beauty in the maze.
With every turn, a new design,
In unseen angles, we align.

Shapes that twist in hidden fight,
Chasing after fading light.
Through the layers, minds we glean,
Unlocking angles of the unseen.

Arc of the Unconscious

In shadows where the whispers dwell,
Unseen secrets begin to swell.
Echoed thoughts collide and dart,
Dancing on the edge of heart.

Fleeting visions drift and sway,
Leading minds in disarray.
Between the lines of waking thought,
Lie the dreams we've dearly sought.

A canvas where all fears conspire,
Flickering flames of lost desire.
Every thread of silence spun,
Forms the arc where we are one.

Beneath the veil of endless skies,
Our hidden truths will always rise.
Connect the dots of dark and light,
In the arc, there shines the night.

Celestial Coordinates

Stars above like wishes cast,
Guiding hearts from first to last.
Celestial maps, a cosmic dance,
Charting souls in timeless chance.

Galaxies whisper, bright and bold,
Stories of the lives they hold.
Nebulas cradle dreams anew,
Painting paths for me and you.

Constellations serve as guides,
Where the universe abides.
Every pinprick of light shown,
Marks the journey we have grown.

In the night, a cosmic sea,
Coordinates of you and me.
Align the stars, let fate align,
In the vastness, love will shine.

Tangents of the Heart

Circles twist, our paths diverge,
In the silence, feelings surge.
Eclipsed by fear, yet still we chase,
Moments lost in time and space.

Hearts like planets, ever-bound,
In their orbits, fate is found.
Distances stretch yet never parts,
Always drawn, we're tangents' arts.

Connections flicker, bittersweet,
In every glance, in every beat.
Navigating through the storm,
Our tangents shift but still feel warm.

Celestial dance, a fragile thread,
Mapping what our souls have said.
In the echoes, love will chart,
The curves and tangents of the heart.

Schemes within a Dream

Where the shadows blend and fold,
Lies a story yet untold.
In the dreaming mind's embrace,
Schemes and plots begin to trace.

Whispers float on moonlit beams,
Woven tightly with our dreams.
Fabric soft as evening sighs,
Holds the essence of our lies.

Time unwinds, reality bends,
Sketching futures, twists, and ends.
Every thought a fleeting wisp,
Caught within the dreamer's grip.

In the twilight, visions gleam,
Chasing echoes, lost in theme.
What is real, what is a scheme?
Life unfolds within a dream.

Chimeras of Space

In the depths where stars collide,
Fleeting shadows softly glide.
Comets paint the cosmic sea,
Whispers of eternity.

Nebulas in colors bright,
Dance beneath the velvet night.
Galaxies in spirals twine,
Echoes of the grand design.

Eclipses weave a silky thread,
Moonlight lingers, softly spread.
Astral dreams begin to stir,
As the cosmos starts to purr.

Lost among the dark expanse,
Wonders lead a timeless dance.
Chimeras dart where shadows roam,
In the void, they've found a home.

The Aesthetics of Asymmetry

In the chaos of a bend,
Beauty lies without an end.
Shapes that twist and turn around,
In their flaws, pure art is found.

Lines that break and bodies skew,
Challenge notions of the true.
In the crooked, we find grace,
Each imperfection leaves a trace.

Angles sharp, yet soft as breath,
Caught in life, beyond mere death.
Harmony in disarray,
Asymmetry leads the way.

From the discord, visions grow,
Unlikely forms begin to flow.
Every curve and every line,
In their strangeness, we define.

Vortices of Imagination

In the whirl of thoughts that spin,
Ideas chase the light within.
Circles swirl, emotions rise,
Dreams emerge with vibrant cries.

Fancies twine like threads of gold,
In the mind, the young and old.
Vortex draws the weary heart,
In its pull, the dreamers start.

Spiraled stories start to weave,
In the depths, we dare believe.
Fiction drifts through endless night,
Lighting paths with purest light.

In the maelstrom, spirits dance,
Lost within the trance of chance.
Vortices swirl, embrace the wild,
In each twist, the soul's a child.

Beyond the Boundaries of Thought

Where the mind dares not to tread,
Lies a realm where dreams are fed.
Thoughts unleash, take timeless flight,
In the dusk before the light.

Whispers echo, truths unfold,
Stories buried, once untold.
Ideas stretch beyond their seams,
Casting shadows on our dreams.

In the silence, wisdom grows,
Life's questions, still no answers show.
Beyond borders, infinite space,
Here we search for our true place.

Limitless the mind's domain,
In each vision, joy, and pain.
Crossing through the unseen gate,
Find the magic, while we wait.

Grids of the Subconscious

In shadows deep, thoughts wander wide,
Through tangled threads, where dreams reside.
Whispers echo, softly play,
Invisible maps that lead astray.

Patterns emerge, a hidden trace,
In silent corners, I find my place.
Veils of silence, secrets unfold,
A tapestry woven, stories untold.

In each square, a memory stirs,
Fragments of time, a dance that blurs.
Lines intersect, paths realign,
In the grid, I find what's mine.

Awake yet dreaming, truth in disguise,
In the heart of grids, wisdom lies.
A canvas rich with colors bold,
In the subconscious, life unfolds.

The Fabrication of Fancies

We weave our wishes in twilight's glow,
Imagined realms where fantasies flow.
With threads of joy, and hints of doubt,
In every stitch, our hopes shout out.

Mirages dance in the mind's embrace,
A symphony played in a delicate space.
Crafting dreams with skillful hands,
Like castles built on shifting sands.

Each whimsy born from a spark of light,
In the dark of night, they take flight.
Flickers of magic in the air,
A tapestry spun from thoughts laid bare.

Yet reality tugs on fanciful seams,
And truth can scatter our wildest dreams.
But still we gather, and stitch anew,
In the fabric of fancies, we find what's true.

Curious Curvatures

Curves that beckon in every glance,
Bending light in an elegant dance.
Whirls and spirals, unpredictable flair,
In each twist, a secret to share.

Sailing through shadows, lightly we go,
Tracing the arcs where soft breezes blow.
Unraveled paths, they whisper and weave,
In the gentle curves, we learn to believe.

The world bends around us, a playful jest,
In every contour, life's little quest.
Revel in shapes that break all the rules,
In curious curvatures, we find the jewels.

So let us glide with the softness of grace,
In every loop, we find our place.
Through the winding paths, let joy be found,
In the art of curves, forever unbound.

The Weft of Whimsy

Threads of laughter, a playful weave,
In the fabric of life, we dare to believe.
Colors collide in a bright array,
In the weft of whimsy, we long to stay.

A dance of silliness under the sun,
Where time stands still, and moments run.
Every stitch a story of joy and jest,
In the tapestry of dreams, we find our rest.

Floating on clouds, in a world askew,
With hearts like kites, we soar anew.
In every flutter, a spark ignites,
From the weft of whimsy, our spirit takes flight.

So gather the threads, let laughter resound,
In this joyful fabric, love can be found.
Embrace the absurd, let your soul roam,
In the weft of whimsy, we build our home.

Intersection of Shadows

In the whisper of the dusk, they meet,
Silhouettes dancing in the retreat.
Fingers of twilight stretch and sway,
In this quiet space where shadows play.

A crossroad of secrets, dark yet bright,
Stories untold in the fading light.
Echoes of laughter, a soft refrain,
Mingle with shadows, dissolving pain.

Ghosts of the past twirl in the night,
Chasing the flicker of a distant light.
Bound by the moment, they swirl in time,
Twisting together, a slow, sweet rhyme.

Where dreams converge in shadows long,
Each heartbeat echoes a silent song.
A canvas painted in shades of gray,
The intersection whispers, come what may.

The Euclidean Odyssey

In a realm where lines and angles meet,
A journey unfolds, intricate and neat.
Geometric wonders soar and glide,
In the Euclidean world, we take pride.

Triangles dance in perfect symmetry,
Circles hum softly, a sweet melody.
Every vertex tells a tale so grand,
In this mathematical wonderland.

Polygons gather in a grand parade,
Each shape unique, none ever fade.
Rectangles march, with elegance and grace,
In this odyssey through time and space.

With rulers in hand, we carve our path,
Calculating angles, avoiding wrath.
Every theorem whispers in the breeze,
The Euclidean quest, a quest to seize.

Spheres Suspended in Air

Floating gently, a spherical dream,
Bubbles of light in a soft silver beam.
Dancing with gravity, defying the ground,
In stillness and silence, magic is found.

Each sphere holds secrets, untold, unseen,
Mirroring worlds in a tranquil sheen.
They drift and collide, yet never despair,
Bound by the beauty of fresh, open air.

With a shimmer of hope, they rise so high,
Carried by wishes that whisper and sigh.
Suspended in moments, they linger and swirl,
In the embrace of the universe, pearls.

Their essence a dance, a harmony clear,
Echoing stories we long to hear.
Suspended in time, they float with delight,
In the vastness of sky, a radiant sight.

Polygonal Pathways to Wonder

Along the paths of edges and lines,
Wonders unfold where the sunlight shines.
Each corner a promise, new worlds to see,
In this polygonal journey, wild and free.

Steps lead us forward, shapes intertwine,
Every turn reveals a new design.
A labyrinth woven with beauty profound,
In geometry's arms, lost and found.

Colors collide where the shapes converge,
Pathways of magic begin to emerge.
Through pentagons' whispers, we venture and roam,
In the heart of the polygon, we find our home.

Curves meet the angles, a symphonic blend,
A tapestry woven, beginning to end.
With each fleeting step, our hearts will discover,
Polygonal pathways to wonder, uncover.

Vectors of the Soul

In the stillness, echoes rise,
Whispers float through endless skies.
They weave through time, they shape the fate,
Drawing paths to love or hate.

Every heartbeat, every sigh,
Connects the earth to stars on high.
In every pulse, a story told,
A dance of warmth in frames of cold.

Dreams become the guiding lines,
Carving hope in unseen signs.
With each turn, the journey glows,
A tapestry of highs and lows.

In silent depths, we learn to soar,
Through love's embrace, we seek for more.
Vectors pulse, and we unite,
Shadows fading, hearts ignite.

Horizons of Hope

Dawn breaks soft on distant shores,
Golden hues rush through the doors.
Every step, a chance to find,
New beginnings, hearts aligned.

In the distance, dreams do swell,
Crafting tales we dare to tell.
Each horizon, a promise made,
Lighting paths where fears do fade.

Gentle winds lift spirits high,
Chasing clouds across the sky.
With every breath, resilience grows,
In the garden where hope flows.

Stars ignite the night's embrace,
In their glow, we find our place.
Horizons wide, we rise anew,
Bound by love, in all we do.

Labyrinths of Light

In shadows deep, the pathways weave,
A dance of light that dares believe.
Each corner turned unveils the truth,
Illuminating dreams of youth.

Winding trails of gold and white,
Guide the lost back to the light.
Invisible threads connect each heart,
Binding souls that will not part.

Whispers echo through the maze,
Filling souls with boundless praise.
In the brightness, fears take flight,
Finding peace in radiant night.

The journey ends, yet still we roam,
In labyrinths, we find our home.
Tracing paths with visions bright,
We're forever in this light.

Luminous Forms

Shapes that shimmer, shadows fade,
In the craft of dreams displayed.
Every color sings a song,
Whispering where we belong.

Echoes of the past resound,
In the spaces all around.
Merging realms of flesh and light,
Luminous forms take their flight.

Transcending time, we come alive,
With every heartbeat, we survive.
In the dance of cosmic grace,
We find a warm, embracing place.

Shapes that shift and gently sway,
Hold the promise of the day.
Luminous forms, a sacred bond,
In the depths, we learn to respond.

Echoes in the Ether

Whispers drift upon the breeze,
Silent songs of ancient trees.
Memories linger in the air,
Echoes call, with gentle care.

Stars alight in velvet night,
Each a dream that takes flight.
Fleeting moments, softly passed,
In the ether, held steadfast.

Time unfolds its tender hand,
Guiding us through shadowed land.
Infinite tales, woven tight,
In the fabric of the night.

Listen close, the secrets shared,
In the silence, hearts laid bare.
Every heartbeat, every sigh,
Echoes whisper, never die.

The Fabric of Fantasies

Threads of hope, spun from desire,
Intertwined, they lift us higher.
In the loom of dreams we weave,
Wondrous tales that never cleave.

Colors bright, both bold and soft,
Patterns shift, as spirits loft.
Each design, a story told,
In the fabric, rich with gold.

Textures merge, a dance of light,
Crafting visions, taking flight.
In the tapestry of night,
Fantasies embrace the sight.

We stand tall in dreams we chase,
In this world, we find our place.
Sewn together, hearts align,
In the fabric, love does shine.

Circles of Connection

In the circle, we find grace,
Every heartbeat, every face.
Bound by stories, shared and true,
In this web, I connect with you.

Hands from different paths entwine,
Support each other, hearts combine.
In this circle, trust will grow,
Endless currents, love will flow.

Each voice adds a unique sound,
Harmony in unity found.
As we dance, we rise and fall,
In this circle, we are all.

From the whispers, we learn to soar,
Embracing all, forevermore.
In each bond, a story stays,
Circles of connection blaze.

Constellations of Longing

Beneath the night, we gaze above,
Tracing paths of hope and love.
Stars like dreams, they shimmer bright,
Constellations in the night.

Longing etches lines so fine,
In the dark, your heart and mine.
Sparkling whispers on the air,
In the cosmos, longing bare.

Every twinkle, every sigh,
Messages sent from you and I.
Mapping feelings, vast and deep,
In the silence, secrets keep.

Wishes cast on cosmic winds,
In this dance, the journey begins.
Together, we will always find,
Constellations of the mind.

The Spectrum of Being

In the light of dawn's embrace,
Colors blend in softest grace.
Shadows dance on fleeting ground,
Whispers of existence sound.

From crimson hues to azure skies,
Every shade a truth that lies.
In the heart, a canvas wide,
Life's true colors, here reside.

Vivid dreams and muted sighs,
In between, the spirit flies.
Each moment, a brushstroke bold,
Paints the stories yet untold.

Embrace the chaos, hold it near,
In every hue, there's love and fear.
Life's rich tapestry unfurls,
A spectrum bright, a dance of worlds.

Lines Drawn in Dreams

In twilight's hush, the mind takes flight,
Sketching visions in the night.
Where the boundaries softly blur,
And the heart begins to stir.

Lines emerge from shadows deep,
Whispers of the soul's own keep.
Beyond the veil of waking time,
Dreams unfold in silent rhyme.

Every scribble holds a key,
Unlocking realms of what might be.
In this dance of light and dark,
We find the flame, we find the spark.

So let the dreams guide our way,
In their embrace, we'll long to stay.
Lines drawn softly in our hearts,
A tapestry where magic starts.

The Arc of Awakening

From slumber's grip, the spirit wakes,
With every breath, the stillness breaks.
Awareness blooms like morning dew,
Illuminating all that's true.

In the space where silence breathes,
Seeds of wisdom, time bequeaths.
Each moment, a divine embrace,
Guiding us to sacred space.

Embrace the journey, feel its flow,
With open hearts, we come to know.
The arc of life, a gentle bend,
Where beginnings meet their end.

Awakening involves the whole,
A dance of body, mind, and soul.
Rising with the sun's first ray,
Finding light within the day.

Parallels and Perceptions

Two worlds run side by side,
In each, the hidden truths abide.
What we see is just a part,
A window to the beating heart.

Mirrored visions, shifting shades,
In the silence, knowledge wades.
Perceptions twist in twilight's hand,
Crafting stories, vast and grand.

In each parallel, lessons grow,
Paths diverge, yet hearts still flow.
What we seek lies deep within,
In understanding, we begin.

So walk the lines with gentle grace,
Discover depths in every space.
For in the dance of minds and dreams,
Truth resides in subtle beams.

Chasing Shadows in Silhouette

In twilight's embrace, shadows play,
Dancing softly, then fading away.
Figures of thought in the dimming light,
Echoes of whispers, lost in the night.

Fleeting moments, like breath on glass,
In the silent chase, time seems to pass.
Reflections of dreams, elusive and shy,
Woven in stillness, beneath the sky.

With each step taken, the shadows shift,
Unraveling stories, our hearts they lift.
A tapestry woven in shades of gray,
Chasing those whispers that fade into day.

Embracing the dance, the joy, and the pain,
In silhouettes cast, there's much to gain.
Though shadows may linger, they teach us to see,
The beauty in darkness, where light longs to be.

The Unseen Framework

Within the structure, unseen yet clear,
Lies a foundation, steady and near.
Bound by the threads of what cannot be seen,
A web of connections, strong and serene.

In silence, it whispers, the truth we ignore,
Building the lives we yearn to explore.
Formations of thought, like roots intertwine,
Interlaced destinies, yours and mine.

Though hidden from view, it shapes our design,
The fabric of dreams, with purpose divine.
Lines of creation that guide our intent,
A map of existence, eternally bent.

In the heart of the unseen, we search for our place,
Navigating chaos with elegance and grace.
For in every structure, there lies a refrain,
A chorus, a journey, a sweet, silent gain.

Divergent Dreams

Winds of ambition blow strong and free,
Carrying visions that long to be.
Like rivers that twist and turn away,
Divergent dreams dance in bright array.

Each path we tread is uniquely our own,
Crafted from moments, in silence grown.
Dreams intertwine, then scatter like seeds,
Sprouting new journeys, fulfilling our needs.

Yet fear may linger, a shadowy trace,
Haunting the corners of hope's gentle space.
But with every heartbeat, we dare to embrace,
The divergent roads that form our own pace.

In the tapestry of life, colors collide,
Blending and swirling, in passion we ride.
For dreams may diverge, like stars in the night,
But together they shine, a captivating light.

Spiraling Journeys

In the dance of life, we spiral and turn,
Each twist a lesson, each flicker we learn.
Horizons stretch wide, inviting our quest,
As we weave our stories, never at rest.

Through valleys and mountains, we wander with grace,
Carving out pathways, embracing each space.
With hope as our compass, we journey ahead,
Finding the light in the paths that we tread.

In circles we gather, then scatter like leaves,
Connected by whispers that fate always weaves.
As seasons collide, and dreams intertwine,
We spiral onward, in rhythm divine.

So take my hand softly, let's twirl and explore,
Infinite journeys await us ashore.
For in the spirals of life, we will see,
The beauty of living, just you and me.

Tangents of Tranquility

In the quiet of dawn's embrace,
Soft whispers dance in the air,
Nature unfolds its gentle grace,
Peace lingers softly everywhere.

Flowing rivers, a tranquil stream,
Birds in chorus, a morning song,
In this moment, one can dream,
Where all the heartbeats belong.

Beneath the shade of ancient trees,
Time stretches like shadows at play,
With every breath, a tender ease,
In stillness, worries drift away.

The world slows down, a sigh released,
In harmony, spirits unite,
From chaos found, a solace feast,
In tangents drawn, we seek the light.

Dimensions of Desire

In the heart's chamber, dreams reside,
Each longing shines, a vibrant hue,
Across the canvas, hopes abide,
Where passions spark and skies turn blue.

Threads of yearning weave their way,
Through shadows, whispers, night and day,
In every glance, a secret play,
In silence, love finds words to say.

Time collapses, moments blend,
In a world where wishes wake,
With every heartbeat, messages send,
Through every choice, the paths we make.

These dimensions stretch and twist,
In a dance of fate, we find,
In every heartbeat, an untold risk,
A tapestry of the intertwined.

Chasing Euclidean Echoes

In a realm where lines bend and break,
We trace the path of the unknown,
Chasing whispers, our hearts awake,
In geometries, we find our own.

Every angle telling a tale,
Of love and loss, of stars that fall,
In spirals where emotions sail,
In symmetry, we hear the call.

Compasses guide our dreams afar,
As we journey through curves and planes,
In the shadows of a distant star,
We seek the beauty in our chains.

Euclidean echoes softly ring,
In the fabric of time and space,
Every heartbeat the answers bring,
In these patterns, we find our place.

The Prism of Possibility

Beyond the spectrum, colors blend,
In every shade, a world takes flight,
A prism shines, where dreams suspend,
In every glance, a spark ignites.

Light refracts through life's design,
Creating hues of joy and strife,
In the moments that intertwine,
We glimpse the vastness of our life.

With open hearts, we dare to see,
The spectrum stretched across the sky,
Each fragment holds a mystery,
In possibility, we reach high.

In the dance of light, we embrace,
The infinite paths that lie ahead,
Through the prism, we find our place,
In every dream, our spirits fed.

Patterns in the Twilight

Shadows dance on twilight's stage,
Each flicker tells a muted tale.
Colors blend, a soft presage,
As night unfolds its velvet veil.

Whispers woven in the air,
Echoes of a day gone by.
Stars begin their gentle stare,
Painting dreams across the sky.

Footsteps traced in fading light,
Marking paths we've yet to tread.
In the hush of coming night,
Silent wishes softly spread.

Heartbeats pulse like distant drums,
In the twilight's tender embrace.
Magic in the silence hums,
Unfolding wonders in this space.

The Blueprint of Reverie

In a dream where shadows play,
Thoughts collide like stars at dawn.
Maps of hopes in vast array,
Sketch the places we have drawn.

Time slips through like grains of sand,
Each moment crafted, pure and clear.
In this realm we take a stand,
Where reality feels near.

Visions swirl like autumn leaves,
Bursts of color weave and spin.
Within our hearts, a story breathes,
A wonder where the dreams begin.

Pages turning, whispers flow,
Creating paths that we will roam.
The blueprint of what we can know,
Is etched within our minds' own dome.

Fractals of Memory

Memories swirl in fractal forms,
Infinite patterns, shapes arrayed.
Echoes of laughter, silent storms,
Time's tapestry carefully laid.

In the maze of yesteryears,
Moments spiral, intertwine.
Nostalgia dances, conquers fears,
In the heart's intricate design.

Each recollection, a piece of art,
A vibrant hue on life's great wall.
Threads of joy and pain will chart,
The journey that unites us all.

Looking back, we seek to find,
The beauty woven in our past.
In fractals rich, our lives aligned,
Echoing truths that ever last.

Curved Reflections

Rippling water holds the sky,
Curved reflections, worlds entwined.
In its depths, secrets lie,
Whispers of what's undefined.

Branches sway in gentle breeze,
Dancing light on tranquil waves.
Nature sings with perfect ease,
A melody that gently saves.

Time itself seems to bend here,
Mirroring dreams as they pass.
Every moment crystal clear,
In the glassy surface, vast.

Curved reflections, truths revealed,
In the harmony of sight.
Through this lens, our fate is sealed,
Embracing shadows, holding light.

Vistas Beyond the Veil

In twilight gleam, the shadows play,
Whispers of dreams, they dance and sway.
Mountains rise beneath the night,
Guiding souls to distant light.

A river flows with tales untold,
Stars above, like jewels of gold.
Each journey leads to realms unknown,
In the heart, a truth is sown.

Winds of change, they softly call,
Echoes linger, never fall.
Open your eyes, the view unfolds,
Worlds await in stories bold.

Embrace the dawn, the mysteries shine,
Vistas vast, where dreams entwine.
Every step along the way,
Reveals a path where shadows play.

The Canvas of Sleep

Upon the bed of woven night,
Dreams take flight, pure and light.
Brush of stars on canvas wide,
In silent realms, our thoughts reside.

Colors blend in twilight's grace,
Shadows dance, the heart's embrace.
Softly whispers through the haze,
Unraveling the mind's maze.

Morning's touch begins to break,
Painting all that dreams can make.
Flickers of a waking mind,
Stories left behind, unwind.

Yet as the day claims the night,
Echoes of dreams fade from sight.
On a canvas vast and deep,
Life unfolds, the secrets keep.

Shadows in Perspective

Figures dance in the evening hue,
Shadows long, with tales anew.
Each angle holds a whispered line,
Echoes flicker, intertwine.

In corners dark, where secrets dwell,
Stories weave a silent spell.
Shapes that shift and softly blend,
Offer views that gradually bend.

Eyes perceive what hearts may miss,
In fleeting moments, we find bliss.
A canvas of life's intricate art,
Shadows play a vital part.

Between the light, the dark shall guide,
In every step, we must abide.
Finding truth within the shade,
Shadows in perspective played.

Illusions of Infinity

Endless loops in a cosmic dance,
Time unwinds with fleeting glance.
Stars collide in timeless flight,
Whispers echo through the night.

Mirrored realms of thought and dream,
Beyond the void, where shadows gleam.
Vast horizons stretch and bend,
Where beginnings and endings blend.

A tapestry of fate and chance,
Every moment—a fleeting glance.
In the depths of cosmic grace,
Illusions weave an endless space.

Yet in the heart, we find a spark,
Guiding souls through realms so dark.
Infinite paths, with love aligned,
In the dance of the intertwined.

The Essence of Enigmas

In shadows where secrets dwell,
Mysteries weave a silent spell.
Each whisper holds a hidden truth,
A dance of dreams, a fleeting youth.

Beneath the surface, silence brews,
Echoes of laughter, hints of clues.
Fragments of thoughts like scattered stars,
Illuminate the darkened bars.

The heart beats with a curious pull,
As riddles in twilight start to lull.
We chase the shadows, never still,
The essence lingers, the thirst to fill.

With every question, the world spins slow,
In the labyrinth of the mind we sow.
The enigma's essence, a fragrant breeze,
Whispers of wonder carried with ease.

Quantum Echoes

In the realm of time, we collide,
Moments reshape, no need to hide.
Particles dance in an unseen way,
Whispering secrets night and day.

Each thought we send, a ripple in flight,
Crossing dimensions, igniting the night.
Echoes of laughter, vibration so bright,
Linking our souls in this cosmic delight.

Uncertainty reigns in this fragile space,
Where shadows and light find a delicate place.
Quantum whispers that twist and twine,
Binding the fabric of fate so fine.

In every heartbeat, a universe sings,
Carried by beams on invisible wings.
A tapestry woven of dreams and yearn,
In quantum echoes, the mind will return.

Conic Whispers

Circles of thought in spirals align,
Geometries gentle, a signature sign.
Conic whispers in the air,
Drawing us close, a dance, a flair.

Elipses wrapped in soft embrace,
Paths intertwine in a timeless trace.
Each angle tells a story anew,
Mathematics of dreams in every view.

Parabolas rise and then retreat,
Mirroring journeys, bittersweet.
In the quiet of infinite space,
Conic whispers leave their trace.

With every curve, a mystery sways,
Unfolding within the cosmic plays.
In the hearts of seekers, they guide the way,
Notes of harmony in the light of day.

Subtle Alignments

Stars converge in a whispered decree,
Paths entwined like roots of a tree.
Movements echo, a cosmic ballet,
Subtle alignments guide every way.

In the stillness, energies flare,
Mirrored intentions find their pair.
Beneath the surface, a current sings,
Weaving together the tapestry of things.

Celestial bodies pulse and sway,
In harmony, they find their play.
Fractions of moments merged as one,
Subtle alignments, a dance begun.

Each heartbeat echoes in the void,
Cradled by fate, destiny employed.
In the quiet, secrets intertwine,
Subtle alignments, a force divine.

Dancers in the Dark

In shadows deep, they sway and twirl,
A silent song, a hidden whirl.
With whispered breaths, the night ignites,
As dancers move in subtle flights.

The moonlight casts a silver thread,
In every leap, a tale unsaid.
They spin like dreams beyond our sight,
In darkened realms, they find their light.

Their spirits free, they break the chains,
In twilight's arms, they feel no pains.
With every step, the world melts away,
In the dark, they wish to stay.

A harmony of souls unbound,
In muted grace, they dance around.
The night their stage, the stars their cue,
In darkness deep, their love shines through.

The Symphonic Shape

In corners sharp, where silence grows,
The music flows, where stillness knows.
A shape emerges, bold and clear,
In tones that echo far and near.

With curves that sway, like winds of spring,
A symphony in everything.
Each note a brush, each pause a stroke,
A canvas where the heart awoke.

Melodies dance through open skies,
In every rise, a sweet surprise.
The rhythm pulses, deep and vast,
A connection forged, forever cast.

In this embrace of harmony,
A shape of dreams, a reverie.
Where sound and sight begin to blend,
In symphonic shape, the journey bends.

Chords of Creation

From silence deep, a whisper starts,
As galaxies align in hearts.
With every strum, a world unfolds,
In chords of life, the story holds.

The notes cascade like rivers wide,
Creating paths where dreams abide.
In every sound, a spark ignites,
In chords of creation, pure delights.

From gentle hums to thunder's roar,
The universe sings forevermore.
Each pitch a breath, a sweet embrace,
In sacred rhythm, time and space.

Together we weave this cosmic thread,
In unity, where all are led.
Through chords and time, our voices rise,
In this creation, love never dies.

The Fusion of Form

In shadows blend, where colors meet,
A fusion blooms, both strong and sweet.
Shapes intertwine, a dance divine,
In every curve, a story's line.

With every edge, a whisper calls,
In textures soft, the spirit falls.
The melding worlds where forms collide,
In this embrace, we shall confide.

A tapestry of varied hue,
In harmony, the old and new.
With every form, a life reborn,
In fusion's touch, we break the scorn.

Together we rise, beyond the norm,
In every heart, a vibrant storm.
The fusion of form, a boundless dream,
Creating futures, as one we beam.

Milton Keynes UK
Ingram Content Group UK Ltd.
UKHW020145221024
449793UK00019B/40